Poems About EMOTiONS

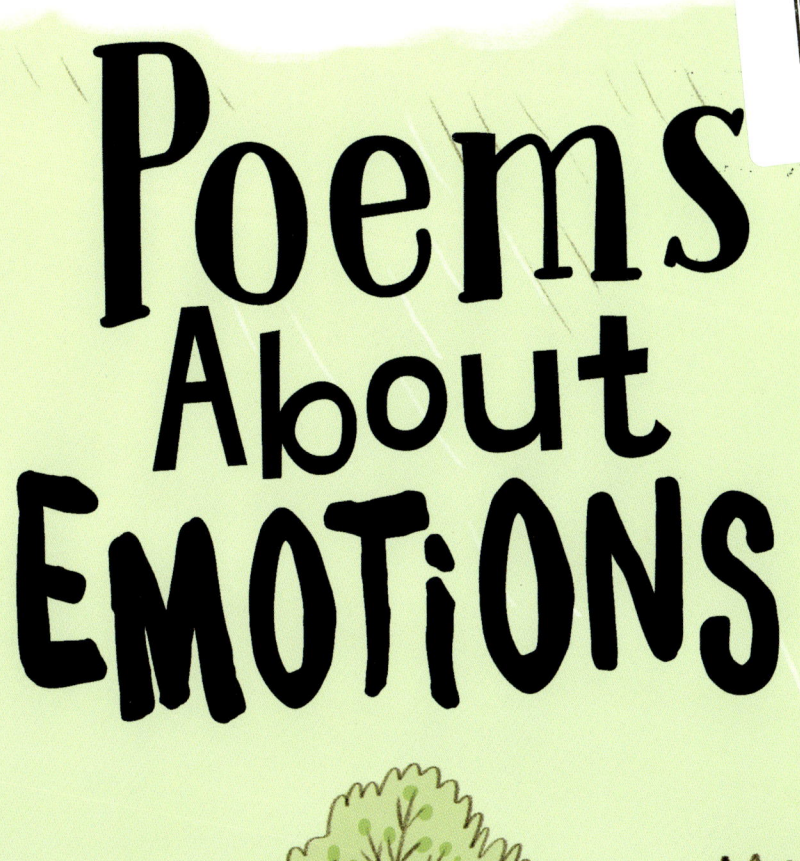

Illustrated by Éva Chatelain

Chosen by Brian Moses

WAYLAND
www.waylandbooks.co.uk

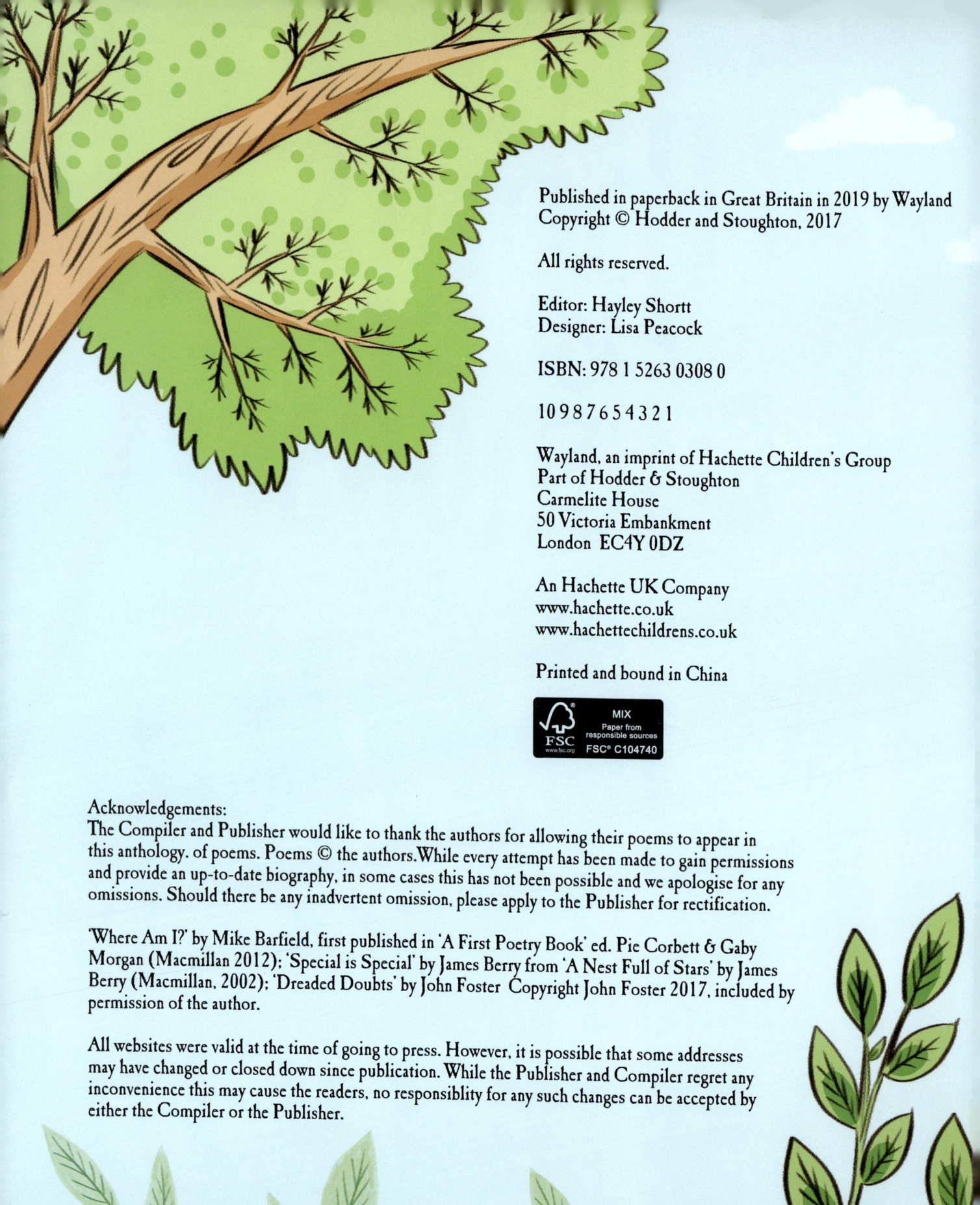

Published in paperback in Great Britain in 2019 by Wayland
Copyright © Hodder and Stoughton, 2017

All rights reserved.

Editor: Hayley Shortt
Designer: Lisa Peacock

ISBN: 978 1 5263 0308 0

10 9 8 7 6 5 4 3 2 1

Wayland, an imprint of Hachette Children's Group
Part of Hodder & Stoughton
Carmelite House
50 Victoria Embankment
London EC4Y 0DZ

An Hachette UK Company
www.hachette.co.uk
www.hachettechildrens.co.uk

Printed and bound in China

Acknowledgements:
The Compiler and Publisher would like to thank the authors for allowing their poems to appear in this anthology. of poems. Poems © the authors. While every attempt has been made to gain permissions and provide an up-to-date biography, in some cases this has not been possible and we apologise for any omissions. Should there be any inadvertent omission, please apply to the Publisher for rectification.

'Where Am I?' by Mike Barfield, first published in 'A First Poetry Book' ed. Pie Corbett & Gaby Morgan (Macmillan 2012); 'Special is Special' by James Berry from 'A Nest Full of Stars' by James Berry (Macmillan, 2002); 'Dreaded Doubts' by John Foster Copyright John Foster 2017, included by permission of the author.

All websites were valid at the time of going to press. However, it is possible that some addresses may have changed or closed down since publication. While the Publisher and Compiler regret any inconvenience this may cause the readers, no responsiblity for any such changes can be accepted by either the Compiler or the Publisher.

Contents

Face to Face *by James Carter*	4
Wonder *by Penny Kent*	5
How Are You Feeling Today-yay? *by Kate Williams*	6
Special is Special *by James Berry*	8
In The Happiness of All *by by Jasimuddin*	9
What's My Name? *by Roger Stevens*	10
Where Am I? *by Mike Barfield*	12
The Dreaded Doubts *by John Foster*	13
KEEP OUT OF MY WAY! *by Clare Bevan*	14
Somebody Else *by Brian Moses*	16
The Grouchy Song *by Joshua Seigal*	18
ANGRY DAY *by Alison Chisholm*	19
Sulking *by Nick Toczek*	20
Bottled Up *by Laura Mucha*	21
Courage *by Penny Kent*	22
Homesickness *by Debra Bertulis*	23
Zip Wire *by Ed Boxall*	24
Worries *by Brian Moses*	26
My Dog *by Marian Swinger*	28
If Feelings Were Flavours *by Kate Williams*	29
Further information	30
About the poets	30
Index of first lines	32

Face to Face

Show me
your sad face.
      Your I-don't-
understand face.
Now do
your lazy face.
      Your cutesy-wutesy
baby face.
Your dreamy face.
      Your sleepy face.
Your me, I-know-
a-secret face.
      Okay, try
your cheeky face.
Your crazy-bonkers
freaky face.
      Your frumpy-grumpy
angry face.
And finally ...
your happy face!

James Carter

Wonder

I'm full of wonder when I find

a feather of the smoothest grey
and softest fluffy white.

I'm full of wonder when I see

a harvest moon as gold as corn
that glows in the autumn night.

I'm full of wonder when I smell

wild, high waves that crash and foam
as they pour towards the land.

I'm full of wonder when I hold

a glittering beetle, shiny green
with spiky legs that tickle my hand.

Penny Kent

How Are You Feeling Today-yay?

Action or facial expression rhyme

How are you feeling today-yay?
How are you feeling today? [CHORUS]

[Clap and swing to the beat, finishing with palms up, as if questioning]

I'm feeling merry as sunshine,
merry as sunshine today.

[Smile, stretching out arms like sun's rays]

[CHORUS]

I'm feeling sad as a raindrop,
sad as a raindrop today.

[Look sad, shaping a raindrop with cupped hands]

[CHORUS]

I'm feeling cross as a big, black cloud,
cross as a cloud today.

[Frown, shaping a cloud with curved arms]

[CHORUS]

I'm feeling wild as the whirling wind, wild as the wind today.

[CHORUS]

I'm feeling calm as a sunset, calm as a sunset today.

[Look excited, swinging arms high each way]

[Smile, spreading arms out smoothly]

Kate Williams

Special is Special

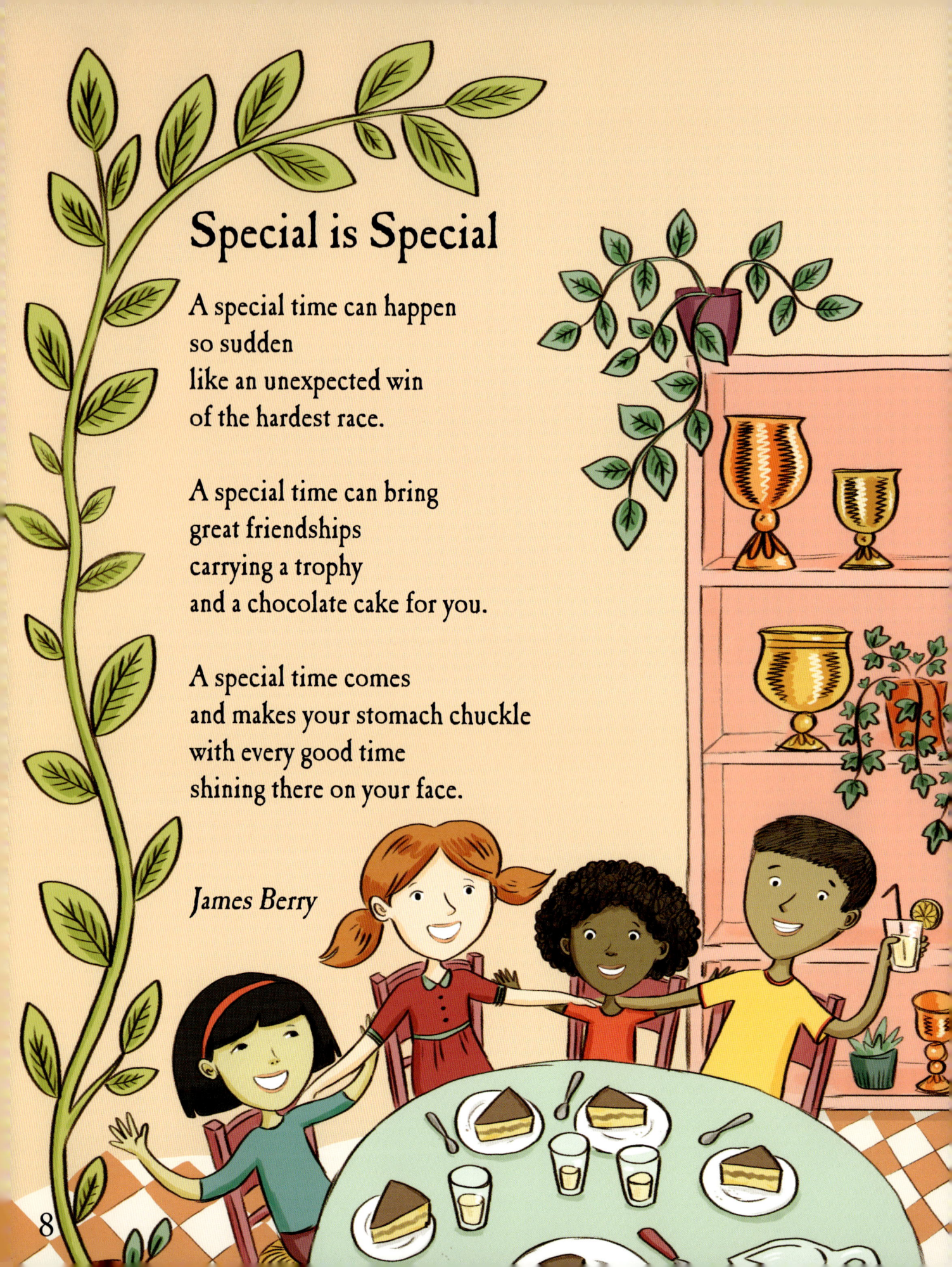

A special time can happen
so sudden
like an unexpected win
of the hardest race.

A special time can bring
great friendships
carrying a trophy
and a chocolate cake for you.

A special time comes
and makes your stomach chuckle
with every good time
shining there on your face.

James Berry

In The Happiness of All

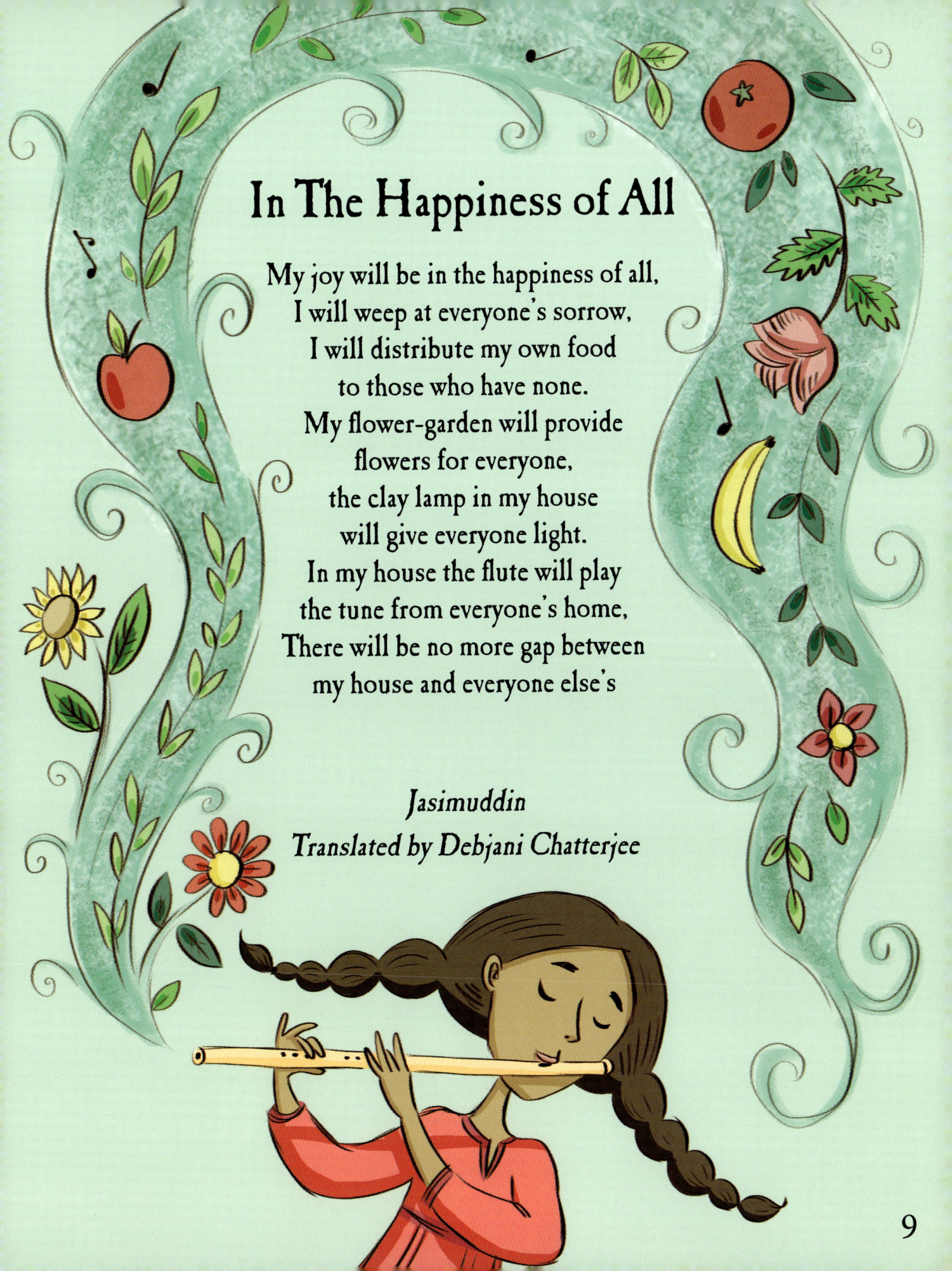

My joy will be in the happiness of all,
I will weep at everyone's sorrow,
I will distribute my own food
to those who have none.
My flower-garden will provide
flowers for everyone,
the clay lamp in my house
will give everyone light.
In my house the flute will play
the tune from everyone's home,
There will be no more gap between
my house and everyone else's

Jasimuddin
Translated by Debjani Chatterjee

What's My Name?

I'm the sun that lights the playground before the day begins

I'm the smiles when teacher cracks a joke. I'm the giggles and the grins

In assembly I'm the trophy that the winning team collects

In your maths book I'm the page of sums where everyone's correct

I'm the pure blue sky and leafy green that wins the prize in art

I'm steamy, creamy custard dribbling down cook's jam tart

I'm the noise of playtime rising through the stratosphere

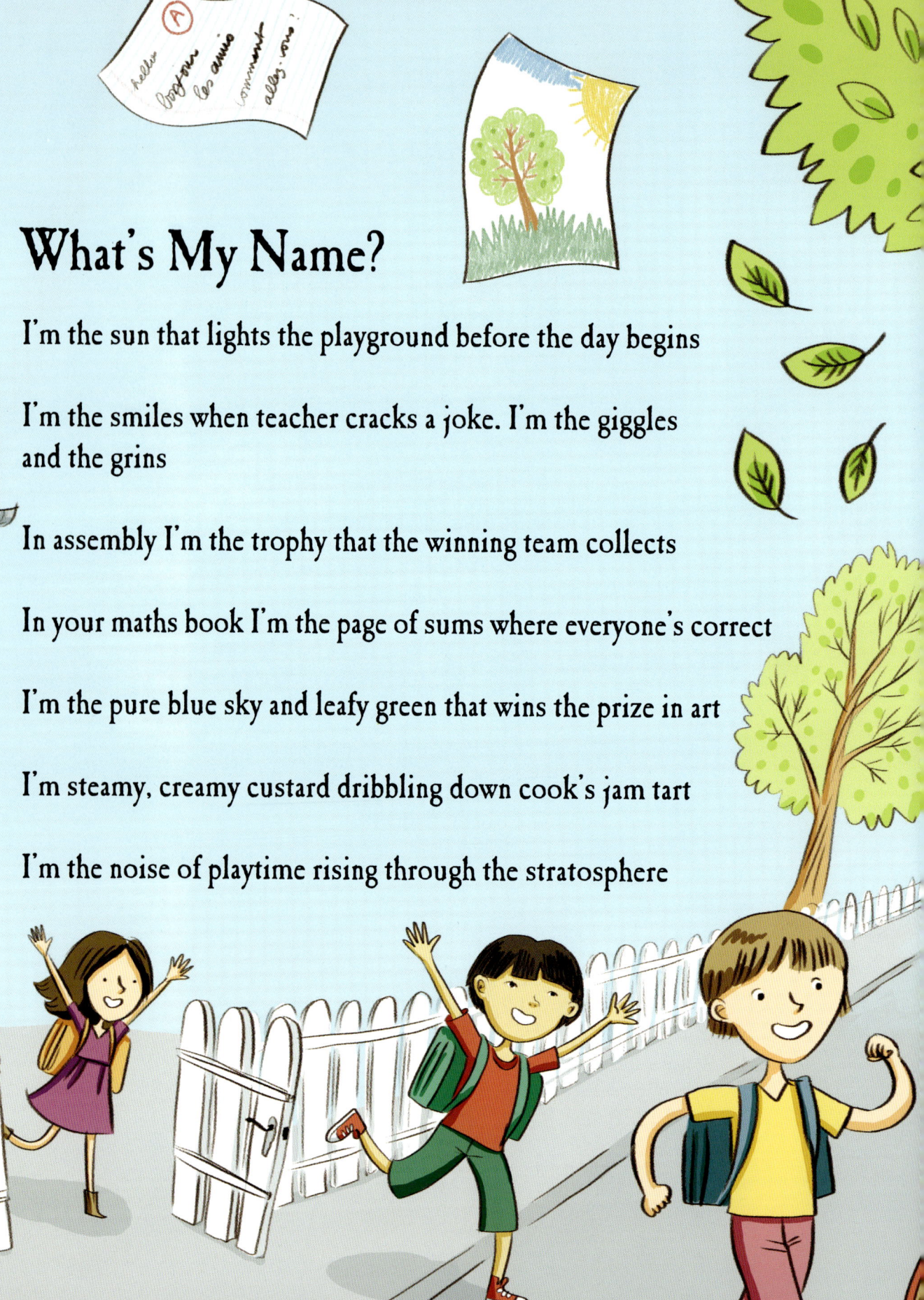

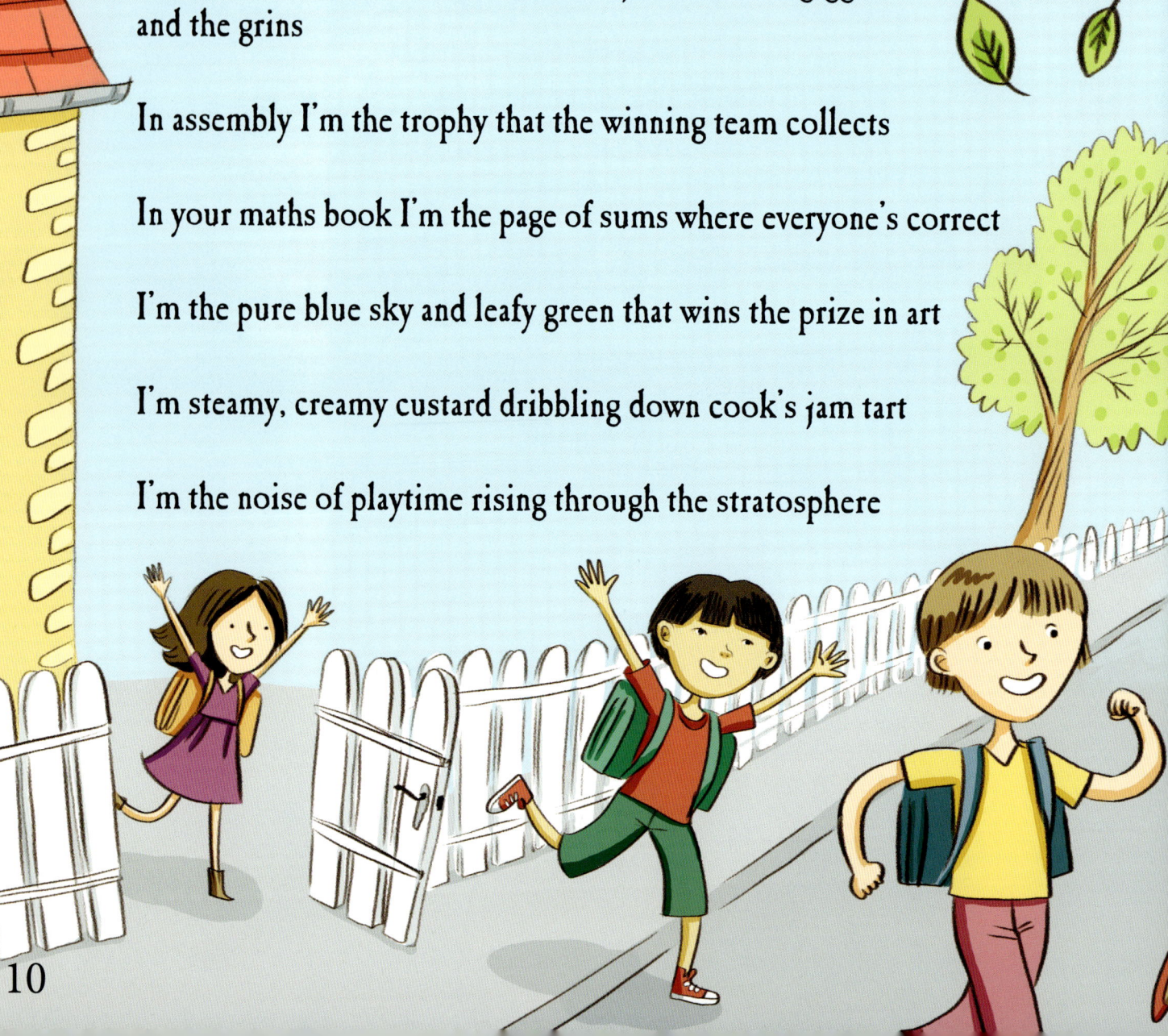

I'm the act of kindness when you lent your kit to Mia

I'm the star you were awarded for your startling poetry

I'm the school gates swinging open on the stroke of half-past three

If you look for me, you'll find me. What's my name?

Can you guess?

I'm just around the corner and my name is

Happiness.

Roger Stevens

Where Am I?

I'm not feeling happy.
I'm not feeling sad.
I'm exactly halfway between
Gloomy and glad.

I'm not one or the other.
I'm not up, I'm not down.
I'm not smiling a smile.
I'm not frowning a frown.

I'm somewhere in the middle.
A new place I've invented.
It doesn't seem to have a name,
I'm just perfectly contented.

Mike Barfield

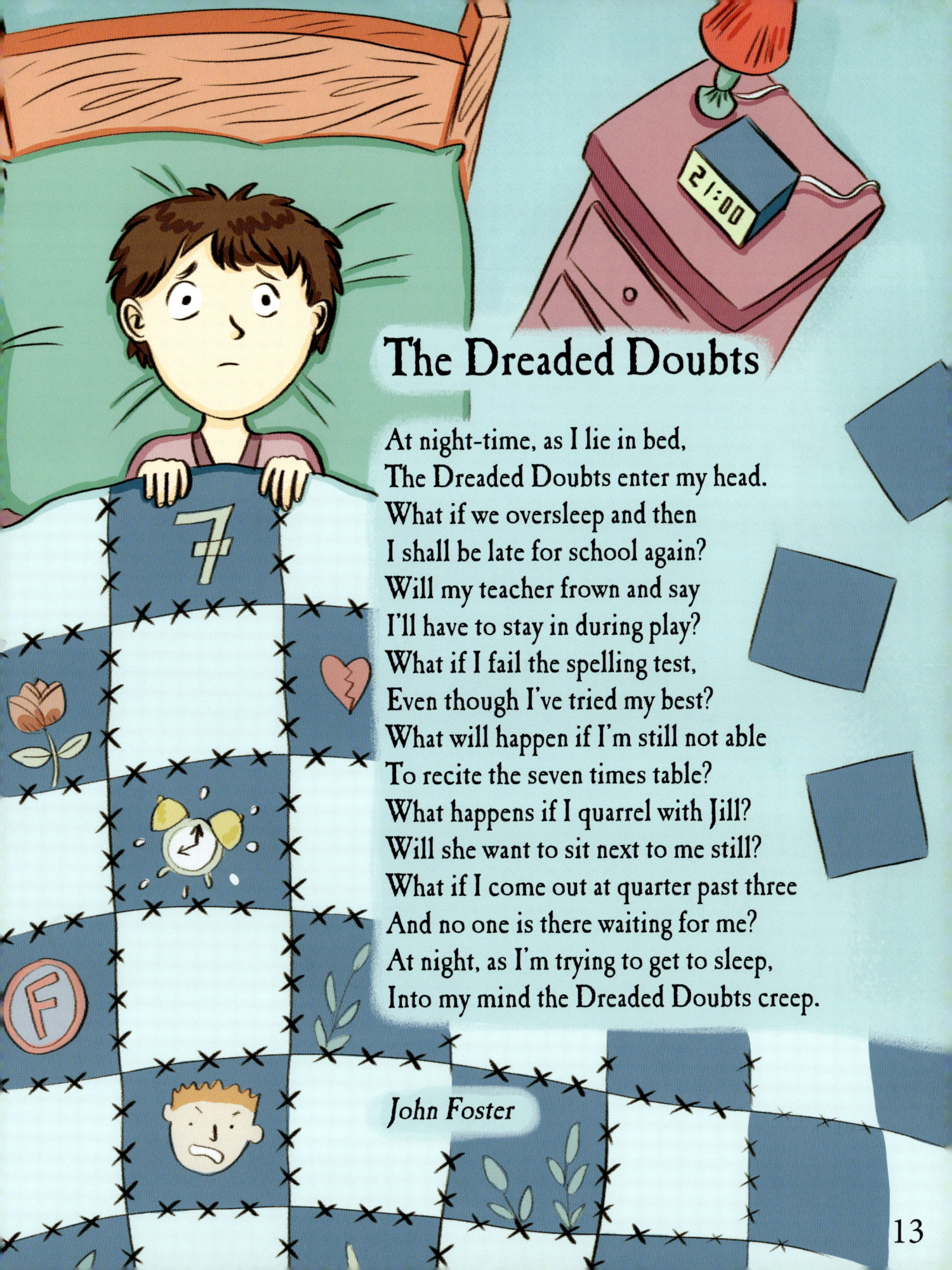

The Dreaded Doubts

At night-time, as I lie in bed,
The Dreaded Doubts enter my head.
What if we oversleep and then
I shall be late for school again?
Will my teacher frown and say
I'll have to stay in during play?
What if I fail the spelling test,
Even though I've tried my best?
What will happen if I'm still not able
To recite the seven times table?
What happens if I quarrel with Jill?
Will she want to sit next to me still?
What if I come out at quarter past three
And no one is there waiting for me?
At night, as I'm trying to get to sleep,
Into my mind the Dreaded Doubts creep.

John Foster

KEEP OUT OF MY WAY!

Keep out of my way!
Keep out of my way!
I'm jealous of EVERYONE today.

If I were a dog
I'd be jealous of a cat.
If I were a mouse
I'd be jealous of a rat.
If I were a circle
I'd be jealous of a square.
If I were an apple
I'd be jealous of a pear.

If I were a bird
I'd be jealous of a bee.
If I were a fly
I'd be jealous of a flea.
If I were a bus
I'd be jealous of a car.
If I were a moon
I'd be jealous of a star.

If I were a bat
I'd be jealous of a ball.
If I were a roof
I'd be jealous of a wall.
If I were a king
I'd be jealous of a clown.
If I were a smile
I'd be jealous of a frown.

I know I'm silly
To feel this way –
But I'm jealous of EVERYONE today.

Clare Bevan

Somebody Else

Who is this somebody else,
who always seems to be
out there, somewhere, some place,
having more fun than me?

Has somebody else got a name,
does she live with her mum and dad,
does she go to bed at the proper time
and is she ever bad?

Does somebody else get measles
on the day before her birthday.
Does she catch a double dose of flu
when she's Mary in the Christmas play?

Is somebody else ever told off
for being unkind to her friend,
or sent up early to bed before
her programme comes to an end?

I think I hate her the most
when we're picking teams in games.
"We're having somebody else", they say
and call me awful names.

But when somebody else is in trouble,
it's then I begin to doubt.
Do I really want to change places
now that her luck has run out?

Brian Moses

The Grouchy Song

If you're grouchy and you know it
give a pout.

> *Hmph!*

If you're grouchy and you know it
start to shout.

> *AHHH!*

If you're grouchy and you know it
stamp your feet and really show it.

Wave your arms
and give a SCREAM
and let it OUT -

> *AHHHHHHHHHH!*

Joshua Seigal

ANGRY DAY

Today I am SO CROSS
I want to ...
    stamp about
    slam doors
    shout at the cat
    get my maths wrong
    stick my tongue out
    break my pencil in half
    yell *knickers* on the bus,
    and throw myself on the floor in the deli
    in a tantrum like my baby sister.

Today I am SO CROSS

but I wish I could remember why.

Alison Chisholm

Sulking

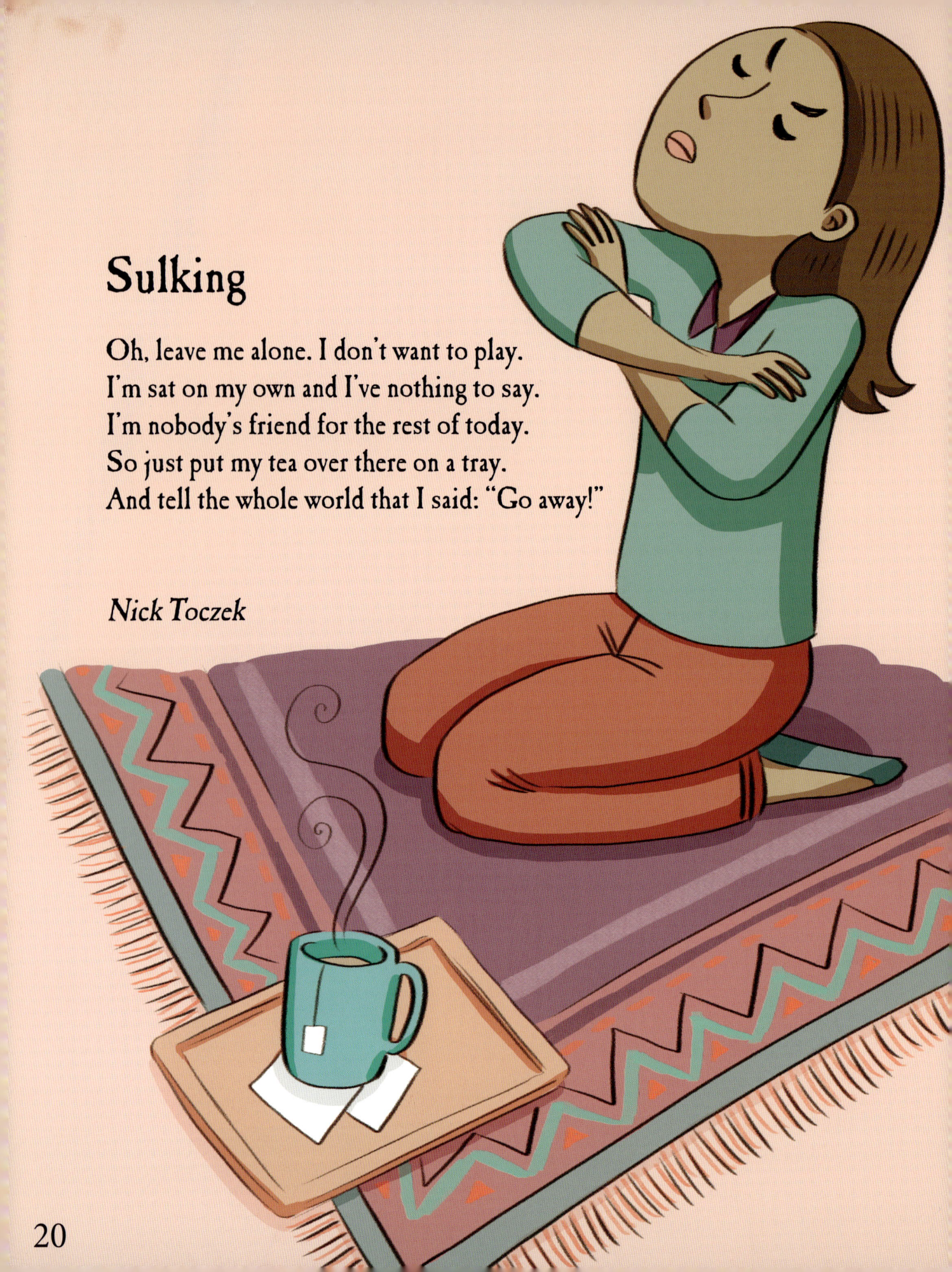

Oh, leave me alone. I don't want to play.
I'm sat on my own and I've nothing to say.
I'm nobody's friend for the rest of today.
So just put my tea over there on a tray.
And tell the whole world that I said: "Go away!"

Nick Toczek

Bottled Up
Laura Mucha

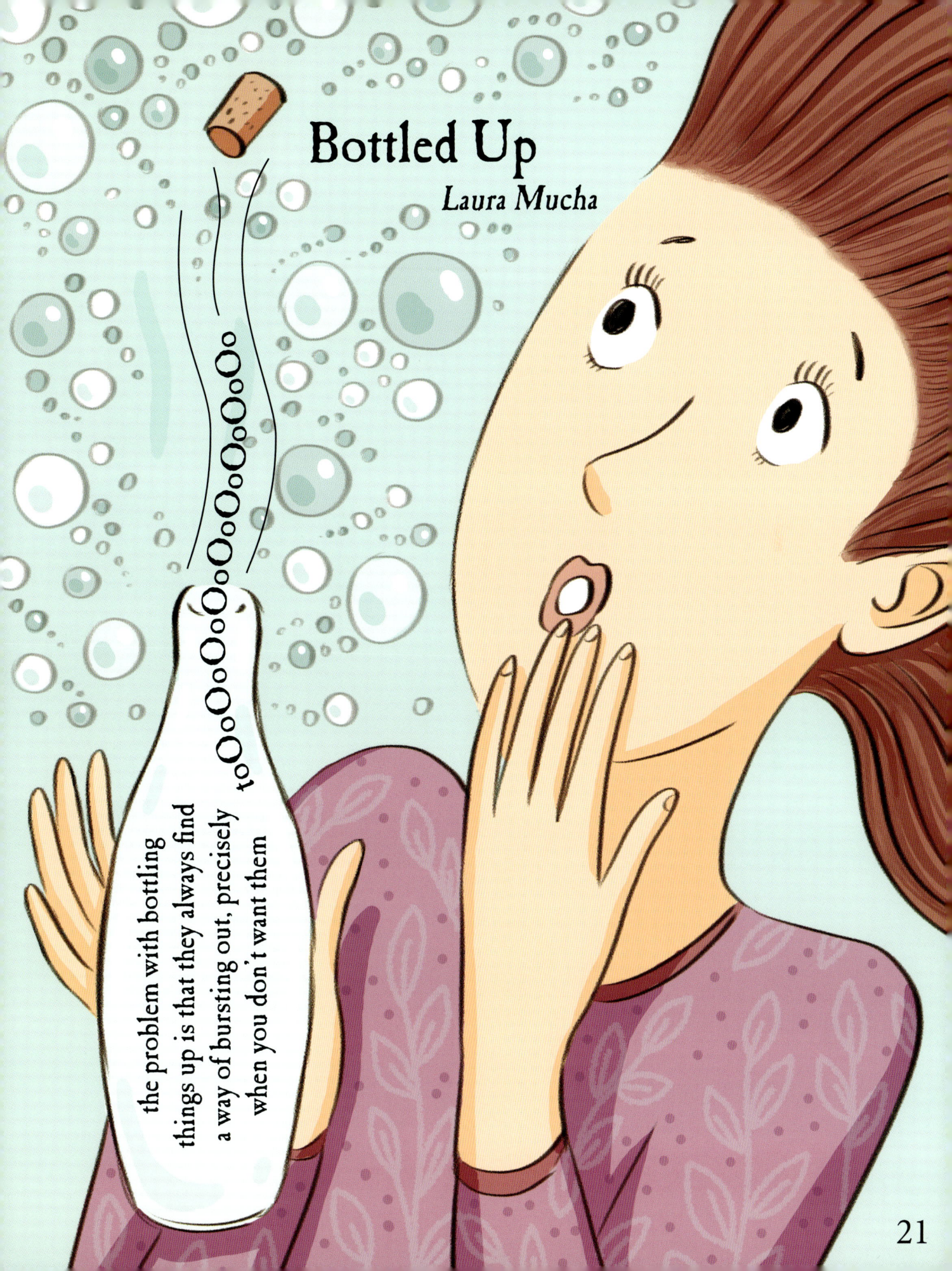

toOoOoOoOoOoOoOoOo

the problem with bottling things up is that they always find a way of bursting out, precisely when you don't want them

Courage

Supriya was brave.
At hometime big kids
were pushing an infant around.
Shoving and taunting
and calling him names.
What a gang.
Lots of children walked by
pretending not to see.
Supriya walked over
and stood in their way.
*Fancy picking on someone
so small*, she said firmly.
The kids were surprised
and while they stood staring
Supriya took the little boy's hand
and walked off with him, quickly.
That took some nerve.

Penny Kent

Homesickness

When Daniel asks me
To his house to play
I sometimes feel homesick
I don't want to stay

My tummy feels strange
And my head really aches
I don't like the feeling
That homesickness makes

But after a while
It just disappears
With my tummy and headache
And all of my tears

It never says goodbye
Just slips quietly away
Whilst Daniel and me
Carry on with our play.

Debra Bertulis

Zip Wire

I will *not* go on the zip wire.

I'm scared,
I don't dare,
I like it here on the swings.

I *will* go on the zip wire.

Look! So high!
Your feet fly,
I love that zip wire zing.

I will *not* go on the zip wire.

Too high,
Don't make me try,
What if I don't fly?

I will go on the zip wire.

I'm scared,
But I do dare,
Everyone else has survived.

I'm scared,
Of big kid's stares,
What if I start to cry?

I *will* go on the zip wire

Oh no,
5 minutes till home
so what if I start to cry?

I am going on the zip wire,

I feel sick,
But I'm doing it,
Here I go ...

ziiiizzzzzZZZZZZZZZZZZZZZZZZZZZZZZZZZZZZZZZZZZZZZZZ

I went on the zip wire!!!

Did you see me?

It was so easy,
Is there time for another ...?

ziiiizzzzzZZZZZZZZZZZZZZZZZZZZZZZZZZZZZZZZZZZZZ

Again!

ziiiizzzzzZZZZZZZZZZZZZZZZZZZZZZZZZZZZZZZZZZZZZ

Just one more go please ...

ziiiiizzzzzZZZZZZZZZZZZZZZZZZZZZZZZZZZZZZZZZZZZ

Ed Boxall

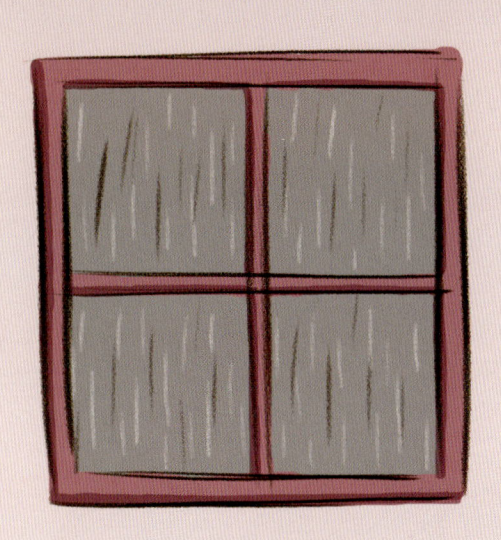

Worries

When my worries weigh me down
I've found a few things I can do ...

I put my worries in a bag
and hide them in
a dark cupboard.

I trundle them away
in a wheelbarrow and leave them
outside the door.

I scoop up my worries
into a net and drop them
into the bin.

I throw them into the sky,
watch them take wings
till they fly, fly, fly
away.

Or I talk to Mum, I chat to Dad,
I stroke the dog, I play with the cat,

then I leave my worries on
the worry mat
and I tell them
not to come back.

Brian Moses

My Dog

Please let her have
just one more day.
That's what I asked Mum.
Just one day, please.
But the vet said she was too old.
In too much pain
and it would be a kindness.
So we had to say goodbye.
But I miss her so much.
I don't want another dog.
I want her.
And what I want to ask,
what I want to know,
is, does the sadness
ever go away?

Marian Swinger

If Feelings were Flavours

Anger would be burning curry,
sizzling with hot spice.

Calm contentment would be sweet -
fudge and all things nice.

Sorrow would be sharp and sour,
fear - cold as ice,
worry – tepid,
horror- putrid,
boredom - bland as rice.

And happiness?
That's so delicious,
you could eat it twice!

Kate Williams

Further information

Once a poem in this book has been read, either individually, in groups or by the teacher, check with the children that they have understood what the poem is about. Ask them to point out any difficult lines or words and explain these. Ask the children how they feel about the poem. Do they like it? Is there a certain section or line of the poem that they particularly enjoy?

'Face to Face' by James Carter is perfect for acting out. Children can devise facial expressions to all the ones that James writes about, and then maybe think of some more. When children have read Penny Kent's poem 'Wonder', they can be asked about what fills them with wonder. It could be spider webs hung with dew, frosted leaves in winter, sea-smooth pebbles sparkling in the sun, mist filling a valley and so on.

Kate Williams provides instructions for how to perform her poem 'How Are You Feeling Today-yay?'. Again, other verses could be added through the repetition of 'I'm feeling …'. After reading James Berry's poem 'Special is Special', children could think about what makes them feel special.

In 'The Happiness of All' by Jasimuddin, ask children to think of what they might do to promote happiness in others. What makes someone unhappy and what can be done to change that? Roger Stevens' poem 'What's My Name?' is a template for writing poems about all kinds of emotions.

Read Mike Barfield's poem 'Where am I?' Ask children what makes them feel content. Are children familiar with 'The Dreaded Doubts' in John Foster's poem? What are the things that they worry about? Link this with the poem 'Worries' by Brian Moses. Are there special ways in which children get rid of their own worries?

Clare Bevan's 'KEEP OUT OF MY WAY!' is another poem that is great for performance, and for writing children's own versions. Discuss the emotions jealousy and envy and relate them to 'Somebody Else' by Brian Moses. Is there always a 'somebody else' who seems to have better luck?

'The Grouchy Song' by Joshua Seigal can be sung to the tune of 'If you're happy and you know it, clap your hands' and 'Angry Day' by Alison Chisholm also explores the emotions of anger and grumpiness. Children can be asked to list the things that make them grumpy and what sort of things help them to calm down?

Children will be familiar with the feelings expressed in 'Sulking' by Nick Toczek and 'Bottled Up' by Laura Mucha. Again, think positively here and ask children to say how they get themselves out of a sulk. They might write down their ideas too:

If I'm sulking it helps if I play with the dog - he always cheers me up - or read a book that takes me to a different place.

Penny Kent's 'Courage' looks at a situation where someone is brave and courageous. Can children think of situations where they've had to be brave? What did it feel like?

'Homesickness' by Debra Bertulis shows a situation with which many children will be familiar. See if there are children who may be able to relate their own experiences of homesickness. Does anything help to lessen that feeling?

Ed Boxall's 'Zip Wire' is an example of a moment of fear, and how it was overcome. Again, children will have their own tales of tell about such moments. Are there strategies that can be put in place for overcoming fear?

In 'My Dog', Marian Swinger writes about sadness caused by the death of a beloved dog. Does the sadness ever go away? It's a difficult area to deal with but some children will already have experienced the loss of a pet and it may be helpful to talk about it.

Make a list of emotions and see if children can add to Kate Williams's ideas in 'If Feelings Were Flavours'. What flavour would courage be, or homesickness, or contentedness?

About the Poets

Mike Barfield is a poet, writer and award-winning cartoonist as well as a rather bad ukulele player. He lives in North Yorkshire. The limericks of Edward Lear along with their grotesque illustrations first got him interested in poetry. An equally abiding interest in science means he can often be seen in schools dressed as a fly performing a show about insects!

James Berry was born in Jamaica, West Indies and came to Britain in 1948. He began writing when he worked as an international telegraphist for British Telecom. He is the author of a number of poetry collections and he won the Signal Poetry Award for his collection *When I Dance* in 1989.

Debra Bertulis' life-long passion is the written and spoken word, and she is the author of many published poems for children. She is regularly invited into schools where her workshops inspire pupils to compose and perform their own poetry. Debra lives in Herefordshire where she enjoys walking in the nearby Welsh hills and seeking out second-hand book shops!
www.debrabertulis.com

Clare Bevan used to be a teacher until she decided to become a writer instead. So far, she has written stories, plays, song-lyrics, picture books and a huge heap of poetry. Her poems have appeared in over 100 anthologies, and she loves performing them in schools. Her favourite hobbies are reading and acting.

Ed Boxall is a writer, illustrator, songwriter and performer. His three favourite things are pizza, islands and unicorns. He would love a pizza as big as an island delivered by a unicorn. His latest book is called *High in The Old Oak Tree*. He's no longer afraid of going on zip wires.
https://edboxall.co.uk/

James Carter is the liveliest children's poet and guitarist in town. He's travelled nearly everywhere from Loch Ness to Southern Spain with his guitar, Keith - to give performances and workshops in schools and libraries and also festivals. An award-winning poet, his titles are published by Frances Lincoln, Macmillan and Bloomsbury.
www.jamescarterpoet.co.uk

Alison Chisholm gets inspiration for her poems from her twin cats Byron and Shelley. When she isn't writing poetry, she's usually to be found reading it or talking about it. Recently retired, she's still trying to decide what to do when she grows up, but as long as it includes poetry she'll be happy.

John Foster is a children's poet, anthologist and poetry performer, well known for his performance as a dancing dinosaur. He has written over 1,500 poems and his anthology *The Poetry Chest* (Oxford University Press) contains over 250 of his own poems. He is a former teacher and the author of many books for classroom use.
www.johnfosterchildrenspoet.co.uk

Penny Kent: For many years Penny enjoyed teaching primary school children from 36 different countries at International Schools in Tanzania, Turkey, Germany, India and South Korea. The range of her cultural experiences is reflected in her children's poems, which have been published in many anthologies. She lives in Gloucestershire now but still travels widely and writes all the time.

Brian Moses lives in Burwash in Sussex where the famous writer Rudyard Kipling once lived. He travels the country performing his poetry and percussion show in schools, libraries and theatres. He has published over 200 books including the series of picture books *Dinosaurs Have Feelings, Too* for Wayland and *Lost Magic: The Very Best of Brian Moses* (Macmillan, 2016).
www.brianmoses.co.uk

Laura Mucha worked as a face painter, studied flying trapeze, and swam in Antarctica before becoming a lawyer. She loves writing poetry for children and was thrilled to win the 2016 Caterpillar Poetry Prize. Her poems have been widely published in magazines and anthologies and she also enjoys performing.
https://lauramucha.com

Joshua Seigal is a poet, performer and educator who works with children of all ages and abilities. He has performed his poems at schools, libraries and festivals around the country, as well as leading workshops designed to inspire confidence and creativity. He has been described by teachers as inspirational and a positive male role model.
www.joshuaseigal.co.uk

Roger Stevens is a children's author and poet who visits schools, libraries and festivals performing and running workshops. He's written lots of poetry books and stories and runs the Poetry Zone, a website for children and teachers www.poetryzone.co.uk He lives in France and England (although not at the same time) with his wife and a very, very, very shy dog called Jasper.

Marian Swinger was born in Lowestoft, Suffolk, but now lives by the Thames in Essex with her partner, son, dog and chickens. For as long as she can remember, she has always loved to paint and draw and to write stories and poetry. She has been a professional photographer for most of her working life and has been writing poetry for children's anthologies for the past 30 years.

Kate Williams When Kate's children were young, she made up poems to read them at bedtime. It was their clever idea that she send them off to a publisher, and she's been contributing to children's anthologies ever since! Kate finds writing a poem is like making a collage, but less sticky – except that she's stuck in the craze! She provides workshops for schools too.
https://poemsforfun.wordpress.com/

Index of first lines

Show me.. 4

I'm full of wonder when I find................................ 5

How are you feeling today-yay?........................... 6

A special time can happen...................................... 8

My joy will be in the happiness of all,................. 8

I'm the sun that lights the playground................ 10

I'm not feeling happy... 12

At night-time, as I lie in bed,................................. 12

Keep out of my way!.. 14

Who is this somebody else,................................... 16

If you're grouchy and you know it....................... 18

Today I am SO CROSS... 19

Oh, leave me alone cos I don't want to play........... 20

the problem with bottling....................................... 21

Supriya was brave... 22

When Daniel asks me.. 23

I will *not* go on the zip wire................................. 24

When my worries weigh me down........................ 26

Please let her have.. 28

Anger would be burning curry,............................. 29